Our
Queen
Remembered

Becky Bishop

Our Queen Remembered

Poems about Her Majesty
Queen Elizabeth II

Other books by Becky Bishop

Poetry
Seasons of Change
Hope can always be found
From the Heart

Strictly Come Dancing
Sequins and Sparkles (2019 series)
Glitz and Glamour (2020 series)
Glitterball Dreams (2021 series)

War Poetry
At The Going Down of the Sun
Lest We Forget

WW2
With all my love, Melvin.

Short Stories
The Adventures of Bluebell Bunny

Facebook: Becky's Poems and Books
Twitter: @Beckypoemsbooks
Instagram: @beckysbijoux
YouTube: Becky Bishop Poems
www.beckyspoemsandbooks.wordpress.com

Dedication

In memory of
Her Majesty Queen Elizabeth II (1926 – 2022)
and
His Majesty The Duke of Edinburgh, Prince
Philip (1921 – 2021)

Dedicated to the Royal Family

Our Queen Remembered

Introduction

Queen Elizabeth II has been a stalwart of our country for over seven decades and the longest reigning monarch in British history which is a remarkable achievement. Throughout her reign she has encountered highs and lows within her family as well as helping the country through good and bad times, the most recent being the covid pandemic, where her words gave hope to so many. Even for those who are not royalists, you cannot help but admire her strength, work ethic, sacrifice and sense of duty and devotion to the crown, her country and commonwealth and her subjects.

On 8th September 2022, the nation was deeply shocked and saddened to hear that Queen Elizabeth II, had passed away aged 96 at her beloved Balmoral home. It is an occasion that people will always remember where they were at the time they heard the news, particularly given that just three months prior we were all celebrating her Platinum Jubilee. Despite her declining health in recent years, particularly since the death of her beloved Philip, when seen in public she has still appeared immaculately dressed and in good spirits. Even two days before her death she was still hard at work, meeting the new prime minister and she appeared quite jolly in pictures from that meeting. That is what makes it so hard to believe that just two days after those pictures were taken she passed away. Following her death there was an outpouring of love for her, with people travelling from across Britain and the world to leave tributes and pay their respects, showing just how much she was admired and respected worldwide.

We now enter a new era under her son, King Charles III and have his coronation to look forward to in 2023. However, the monarchy will never be the same without our beloved Queen.

My family and I are and always have been royalists and have greatly admired the Queen. On the occasion of her Platinum Jubilee I sent her a copy of the poem I had written especially for it, not really expecting a reply back but was thrilled and amazed when I received a reply a few months later. I am also lucky enough to have a photo of the Queen when she was still a Princess visiting RAF Mildenhall with her parents during WW2. Two items that I now greatly treasure.

Our Queen Remembered is a collection of poems written as a lasting tribute to Queen Elizabeth II and as a way to commemorate her life and reign. I hope you enjoy the poems.

God bless our gracious Queen.

God save our King.

Contents

Our Queen Remembered

Prince Philip's death

Prince Philip, the Duke of Edinburgh, has
now sadly passed away,
The nation mourns a man, who supported the
Queen in every way.

Aged ninety-nine, he's led a long and
interesting life,
Throughout it all he's helped the Queen,
through good times and through strife.

As a young man he served in the Navy, he's a
veteran of the war,
And upon joining the Royal Family, he served
his country even more.

In 1947, he made the Queen his wife,
And for seventy-three years, they've shared a
happy and loving life.

A love story that's spanned decades, it's stood
the test of time,
The Queen's companion and rock, he's been
there to help her shine.

A stalwart of the Royal Family, a source of
strength to the Queen during her reign,
Proud of his children and grandchildren,
without him their lives won't be the same.

A lifetime of duty and service, of which he
didn't seem to mind,
Setting up the Duke of Edinburgh award and
supporting charities, a wonderful legacy he
leaves behind.

As the world mourns a man, who was born
the Prince of Greece,
We thank him for his service and may he rest
 in peace.

Prince Philip's funeral

Saturday 17th April, Windsor was bathed in sun and blue skies,
As the Royal Family came together for Prince Philip, to say their final goodbyes.

A military procession, a fitting tribute for a naval and military man,
Before his coffin was placed on the Land Rover hearse and his final journey began.

With his children and grandsons walking behind, for this occasion they united as one,
Before a minutes silence, signalled by the sound of guns.

As he laid in the chapel, to a service of hymns and prayer,
Despite the restrictions, it was a sombre yet beautiful affair.

A service to honour his love and devotion to
his wife and his duty to his country and
Queen,
For the millions watching from home, seeing
the Queen sitting alone was a moving and
emotional scene.

The Queen mourns her beloved soulmate and
husband, someone who was her strength and
stay,
A man who for seventy-three years, was by
her side each and every day.

Now she faces life alone, without Philip by
her side,
But he'll be there as her shadow, a spirit there
to guide.

Their love will still endure, for it's an
everlasting love,
Now he can rest in peace and watch over the
Queen from above.

Platinum Jubilee

A young Princess Elizabeth, so serene and
beautiful,
Even before she was Queen, to her country
she was dutiful.

On 6th February 1952, she acceded to the
throne,
Now the longest reigning sovereign, she's
made the monarchy her own.

Then came the special event, that of her
coronation,
When to her subjects, she swore her
dedication.

A life of service and duty, she's been a
hardworking royal,
To her country and commonwealth, she's
been devoted and loyal.

During her long reign, she's experienced
highs and lows,
But throughout it all, a great strength of
character she always shows.

Helping us through difficult times, with her
words she does inspire,
Always leading by example, she's someone to
be admired.

2022 is a special year, when we'll come
together as a nation,
To mark the Queen's seventy years on the
throne, a cause for great celebration.

The first monarch to celebrate, a Platinum
Jubilee,
A momentous and special occasion, that'll go
down in history.

We send our congratulations, for the long
reign that she has seen,
We thank her for her hard work, God Save
our beloved Queen.

Growing up to be Queen

Playing in the grounds of Buckingham Palace,
when she was a little girl,
A bonny Princess, with a head full of curls.

Elizabeth she was born but Lilibet to her
family,
Surrounded by love, a childhood that was fun
and carefree.

Seeing her father become King, realisation
dawned,
That one day she'd be Queen, on her the
crown would be adorned.

During her teenage years, more royal duties
she had to do,
Before serving in the women's army, during
World War Two.

Finding love with Philip, later becoming his
wife,
Together they negotiated, the ups and downs
of life.

Throughout her reign, he was her strength
and stay,
Always by her side, every step of the way.

A loving mother, to a daughter and three
sons,
Nurturing them through life, showing them
how duty should be done.

On the sad death of her father, Queen she
became,
And for her family, life was never quite the
same.

Over her reign, good and bad times she has known,

But no matter what, strength and dignity she's always shown.

Now as she stands with her family, on the balcony of her childhood home,

Celebrating her jubilee and a remarkable seventy years on the throne.

When Paddington came to tea

2022 was an important year, it marked my
Platinum Jubilee,
And unbeknown to my family, a special bear I
invited to tea.

That bear was called Paddington, who came
from the depths of Peru,
And so he came to Buckingham Palace, to
enjoy a cup of tea or two.

From china cups we drank and had a little
chat,
And then a marmalade sandwich, he
produced from under his hat.

He offered me his sandwich but I had one of
my own,
I always keep it in my handbag, a secret no
one's ever known.

Then the music started, we began to tap our
spoons,
The perfect end, to a wonderful afternoon.

What made it even more special, was seeing
my family laugh and smile,
A moment to treasure, it made it all
worthwhile.

Tribute to Queen Elizabeth II

The world comes together, in memory of a
beloved Queen,
Mourning the loss, of the greatest monarch
we've ever seen.

For seventy years she's reigned, showing duty
and dedication,
And right until the very end, she continued to
serve her nation.

Full of dignity and grace, she was truly one of
a kind,
The end of an era but a remarkable legacy she
leaves behind.

An inspiration and icon, forever she'll remain
in the public's hearts,
Reunited with her beloved Philip, now they're
no longer apart.

For he was there waiting for her, as her time came,
With his hand outstretched, softly calling her name.

Together they'll take their places, on their thrones in heaven's sky,
Watching over her loyal subjects, from a place up high.

Her service is now over, it is her time to rest,
Always showing strength and courage, she was the very best.

She's made her country proud, a role model to so many she's been,
We thank her for her service, God Bless our gracious Queen.

Q.U.E.E.N E.L.I.Z.A.B.E.T.H

Queen of her country, Queen of our hearts,

Uniting her subjects, from the very start.

Entrusted into the role, it was her vocation,

Engaging with the public, serving her nation.

Never failing in her duty, in her country she
had honour and pride,

Excelling in her role as monarch, with her
family at her side.

Loyalty to the crown, from a young age it was
ingrained,

Instilling great values, throughout her
seventy-year reign.

Zero airs and graces, she was kind,
understanding and always cared,

A life lived in the public eye and in the media
glare.

Beaming her beautiful smile, to all those that she met,

Elizabeth, our monarch, a woman we'll never forget.

Tirelessly she's worked, over the seventy years,

Her Majesty, an icon, for whom we'll shed some tears.

A nation mourns its Queen

With their cards and flowers, people come
from far and wide,
Gathering at Royal palaces, to mourn side by
side.

Paying their respects, showing love to the
Royal Family,
Laying their tributes, their grief is clear to see.

Crowds coming together, spanning the
generations,
To say their goodbyes, to the grandmother of
the nation.

A woman who for decades, the country has
admired,
For her dedication to her subjects, many
people she's inspired.

The outpouring of love, shows how much
she's respected and adored,
She'll always be our Queen, now and forever
more.

Dearest Grannie

Dearest Grannie, oh how we love and miss
you so,
And wish with all our heart, that you hadn't
had to go.

We remember all the fun times, we've had
with you over the years,
Now just precious memories, for you we shed
many tears.

You were always there with advice, words of
wisdom you shared,
Making us laugh and comforting us, for all
your grandchildren you cared.

The matriarch of our family, you were our
leader and our guide,
Teaching us life lessons, a role model in
whom we have such pride.

With us in our happy times and in our sad
times too,
Always leading by example, in everything
you had to do.

To us you weren't just our Queen, you were
someone so much more,
For you were the best Grannie, that we could
have ever asked for.

My final journey

From my beloved Balmoral, a favourite place
of mine,
I make my way to London, a journey I make
for the very last time.

In slow procession, I pass the many crowds
that wait,
Ready to pay their respects, as I lie in state.

Draped in the Royal Standard, on my coffin
my crown is placed,
People file past me, grief and emotion on their
face.

For seven decades, I was the nations guide,
And now my loyal subjects, stand vigil by my
side.

Throughout it all my children, have been
beside me every step of the way,
Honouring their matriarch, their love and
pride for me is on display.

My family coming together, in a time of great
distress,
Mourning with the country, as they lay me to
rest.

Soon it'll be time to say goodbye, a goodbye
that'll be my last,
For then it'll be time to cheer for the King, for
my son the flag will fly at full mast.

Then I'll make one last journey to Windsor,
solace and peace I always found there,
A last goodbye to my family, it will be a
private affair.

For then I'll be reunited with my parents and husband, they've been waiting for me,
I will be a Queen no longer, to them Lilibet I'll always be.

Now as my son takes over, on him you'll now depend,
I say a fond farewell, my service and reign is at an end.

A beloved Gan-Gan

In London and Windsor, the Queen's funeral
got underway,
For Prince George and Princess Charlotte, it
was a momentous day.

Walking behind the coffin, with solemnity
and pride,
Reassured by their parents, a constant
presence by their side.

With respectful silence, they sat in their pew,
To say a last goodbye, to the great granny that
they knew.

Showing strength and courage and a maturity
that belied their tender years,
On their best behaviour, to Royal protocol
they did adhere.

Whilst the nation mourned a monarch, a role model and inspirational woman,
To Prince George and Princess Charlotte, she was just their beloved Gan-Gan.

A last goodbye

Thousands lined the streets, millions watched
on TV,
The Queen's state funeral, broadcast for all the
world to see.

With pomp and ceremony, which only the
British do best,
A final farewell to her Majesty, before she was
laid to rest.

The three forces coming together, rehearsing
at night,
So that on the day, they would get it just right.

Standing to attention, their boots and buttons
polished so they'd shine,
Preparing to do their duty, serving their
Queen for one last time.

To the beat of the drum they marched, not a step out of place,
The Royal Family following behind, walking with dignity and grace.

Eight young pallbearers, they were the chosen few,
Carrying Her Majesty's coffin, the most important job they've had to do.

Dignitaries from the Commonwealth, came to pay their respects,
Mourners came from far and wide, on them the Queen's death had a great effect.

With hymns and readings, it was a service to commemorate a long reign and life,
Giving thanks to a woman, who was a loving mother, grannie, great grannie and wife.

Then to the sound of a bagpipe the coffin was
lowered, until it could no longer be seen,
Into the vault to her final resting place, where
she could dream her final dream.

With her husband and parents, she was
reunited once again,
A fitting farewell for a lady, who had an
incredible reign.

Your faithful friends

We were your beloved corgis, we were your
faithful friends,
Your constant companions, right until the
very end.

Our leads in your hands, you used to take us
for many a walk,
Giving us gentle pats, to us you used to talk.

One of our favourite things, was lying at your
feet,
Waiting patiently, for a sneaky little treat.

Things are now different, since the day you
left,
We're missing our mistress, we feel quite
bereft.

Even though you're now gone, to you we'll
always be loyal,
You'll always be our beloved mistress, our
very favourite royal.

Grieving in the public eye

For eleven days the Royal Family mourned in
public, coming together as a family,
But for them their grief was on display, for the
whole world to see.

No chance to grieve in private, dignitaries
they had to meet,
Viewing all the tributes, the public they had to
greet.

Shaking hands and signing documents,
attending services to pray,
Constantly on the go, a busy schedule since
that first sad day.

The grief, strain and sadness, can be seen in
their eyes,
Putting on a brave face in public, doing their
best not to cry.

Now the funeral is over, at last they can grieve
behind closed doors,
Grieving a mother, grandma and great
granny, whom they all adored.

King Charles III

The end of an era, a new one has begun,

A moment Charles knew, that one day would

come.

The accession was announced, in a

proclamation,

An historic occasion, for the first time

broadcast to the nation.

Now no longer a prince, King Charles III is his

new name,

Undertaking new duties, as he commences his

reign.

Taking on his mother's role, he has big shoes

to fill,

Making the monarchy his own, yet upholding

the values she did instil.

Queen Consort Camilla and William, the
Prince of Wales, will be there to help him
through,
Supporting him in his new role and the duty
he has to do.

As the country mourns its Queen, loyal
subjects now await,
To welcome their new monarch, their new
Head of State.

Now for her eldest son, the national anthem
people will sing,
Supporting the new monarch, God Save our
King.

And watching her beloved son, from her
throne above,
Will be our wonderful Queen, looking down
with love.

She'll still be there in spirit, a little voice on his shoulder there to guide,

For even though she's gone, she'll be a constant presence at his side.

King Charles' Coronation

For King Charles' coronation, plans are
underway,
An event to be marked, on the 6th of May.

The first coronation, in the twenty-first
century,
An occasion which will be full of pomp and
ceremony.

Watched on by his family, Charles will be
crowned King,
With Camilla being crowned, Queen Consort
alongside him.

Full of longstanding historic traditions, an
event that'll be watched by the nation,
The country coming together, it'll be cause for
celebration.

Dear Reader

If you have enjoyed reading this book, then please leave a review on Amazon.

Thank you.

Printed in Great Britain
by Amazon

10257793R00031